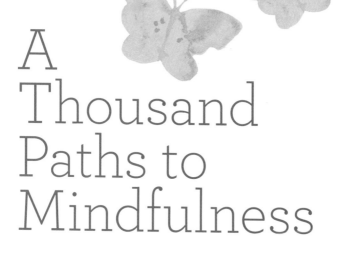

A Thousand Paths to Mindfulness

Liz Dean

An Hachette UK Company
www.hachette.co.uk

First published in Great Britain in 2015
by Spruce, an imprint of Octopus
Publishing Group Ltd
Carmelite House
50 Victoria Embankment
London, EC4Y 0DZ
www.octopusbooks.co.uk
www.octopusbooksusa.com

This edition published in 2018

Distributed in the US by
Hachette Book Group
1290 Avenue of the Americas
4th and 5th Floors
New York, NY 10104
Distributed in Canada by
Canadian Manda Group
664 Annette St.
Toronto, Ontario, Canada M6S 2C8

Some of this material previously ap-
peared in other titles in the *Thousand
Paths* series, also published by Octopus.

ISBN 978-1-84601-573-1

A CIP catalogue record for this book is
available from the British Library

Printed and bound in China
10 9 8 7 6 5 4 3 2 1

Staff credits:
Consultant Publisher: Sarah Ford
Art Director: Jonathan Christie
Designer: Penny Stock
Illustrator: Abigail Read
Editorial Assistant: Francesca Leung
Proofreader: Jane Birch
Production Controller: Sarah-Jayne
Johnson

A Thousand Paths to Mindfulness

Liz Dean

Contents

Introduction

Mindfulness is fast becoming one of the most effective ways to deal with our stressful, busy lives. It's about developing a true awareness of the present moment—letting go of the past and the future, we can experience life more deeply, in the here-and-now. And we don't need to sit cross-legged meditating on our own for hours, because **Mindfulness** is an attitude

that we can practice any time: at home, at work, or while traveling. You can be mindful making a cup of coffee, listening to a friend talk, or while walking—just by paying careful attention to your actions and responses to that task, without your mind wandering.

When starting out on our mindful journey, it helps if we slow down a little, and cultivate patience. We may find ourselves judging ourselves and others less harshly, or not at

all, and begin to accept "negative" thoughts as just thoughts, with no label attached. We become kinder to ourselves, and extend this compassion to others, too.

Then, the world begins to appear differently; we see the same "old" things in a new light, in the spirit of curiosity—like being a child again and discovering everything for the first time. Through **Mindfulness**, we may enjoy all the richness life has to offer.

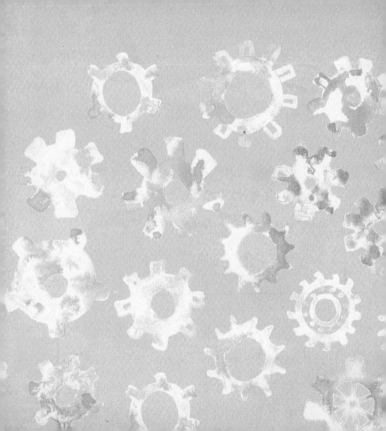

1

Being in the moment

Mindfulness means being awake. It means knowing what you are doing.

Jon Kabat-Zinn

The key to transformation is to make friends with this moment. What form it takes doesn't matter. Say yes to it. Allow it. Be with it.

Eckhart Tolle

Most people will go through life only seeing what they are prepared to see. Mindful people go through life prepared to see it all.

One distracted person takes two hours to do 60 minutes.

The cost of delight is paid with our attention.

Discovery lies not over the horizon, but in the landscape before us. It exists in our developing new ways of looking at it.

Face life with your natural mind, not your conditioned mind.

Feel any way you want,
right now.

Wonder at the
wonder of it all.

The most vital time to
relax is when you don't
have time for it. But you
only need a moment.

Chase butterflies and they will never be caught; watch butterflies and they will come to you.

Trust the moment as it unfolds.

Each moment is extraordinary.

Between the question and the answer lies free choice.

There are those who go through life impatiently waiting for something to happen so that they can start living, and there are those who accept each day as a precious and original gift to be enjoyed.

The little things in life are generally the most important.

Life is a matter of moments; don't be in a hurry for it to be over.

Be still, be patient: this is the greatest strength we know.

The most important moment to be cherished is always now.

Why is the present called the present? Because it is a gift.

In the "now" lies the source of our power.

In the "now" it is possible to change.

The "now" is all that matters.

My friend, let's not think
of tomorrow, but let's
enjoy this fleeting moment
of life.

Omar Khayyam

Observe a moment
in the day without
wanting or not
wanting.

Wake as if for the first
time, and see the world
through fresh eyes.

Love the present.

The only important
moment is now.

Diana Cooper

Every morning
dedicate a moment
to yourself and your
place in the new day.

We all have an
equal share in
possibility.

Look around
you now, at the
things that bring
you joy: a leaf,
your coffee, your
child, a ring, a
photograph, a
fire, a warm heart.

On John Ruskin's desk there was a stone and on it carved the word TODAY.

Happy is he who is not weighed down by the stones of this life.

Human felicity is produced not so much by great pieces of good fortune that seldom happen as by little advantages that occur every day.

Benjamin Franklin

Just for today, you do not have to ask questions or look for answers. With an awareness of the moment, answers are already in front of you.

Look at what is on your plate. Take a moment to appreciate its little details. Where did your food come from? Who were the people who made the ingredients? Put yourself in their shoes. Be thankful. Then, eat.

There's beauty all around our paths, if but our watchful eyes can trace it midst familiar things, and through their lowly guise.

Felicia Hemans

There is beauty at the top of the mountain and in the sunlit plains just as there is beauty in the valley and the deep shadows.

Being in the moment means we are prepared to be with every aspect of our selves.

Reflect upon your present blessings, of which every man has plenty; not on your past misfortunes of which all men have some.

Charles Dickens

Respect each moment—it, and your place in it, is unique and never to be repeated.

The best way to capture moments is to pay attention. This is how we cultivate mindfulness.

Jon Kabat-Zinn

This moment, you don't
need to strive.

This moment, you don't
need fast results.

This moment, you don't
need to judge.

Just be, this moment.

Why wait for some extraordinary circumstances to do good action? Use ordinary situations. Use the moment.

Take pleasure from the past, but live in the now.

The pessimist feels the wind and fears a hurricane.

The optimist feels the wind and waits for the change.

Me? I fly my kite.

Sit in reverie, and watch the changing color of the waves that break upon the idle seashore of the mind.

Henry Wadsworth Longfellow

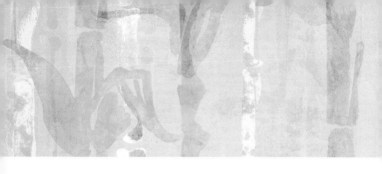

What lies behind us
and what lies before
us are tiny matters,
compared to what
lies within us.

Ralph Waldo Emerson

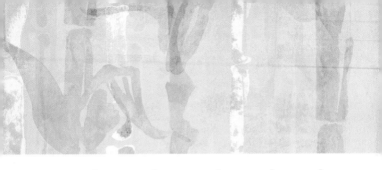

Love what is; leave alone thoughts of what may be.

In essence, you and what we call the present moment are, at the deepest level, one.

Eckhart Tolle

37

Once life becomes a habit we cease to learn.

When our habits deprive us of curiosity, we are mindless.

When we experience our old habits in a new way, we are mindful.

Often the most precious moments in life are made by the simplest things, like buying a glass of lemonade.

Most of the trouble in our lives never actually happens.

Be like a child. For children, every moment and every thing is brand new.

Today, open your eyes as if for the very first time. What do you see?

Accept your weight this moment.

Accept your talents this moment.

Accept your relationships this moment.

Accept who you are this moment.

Pay attention to the coolness of the wind or the warmth of the sun on your cheeks, and smile.

In the name of God, stop a moment, cease your work, look around you.

Leo Tolstoy

The more I give myself permission to live in the moment and enjoy it without feeling guilty or judgmental about any other time, the better I feel about the quality of my work.

Wayne Dyer

Instead of focusing on what needs to be done, turn your attention to what you can create with the moments you are given.

The crowded hours come to you always one moment at a time.

When you dance, the object is not to get to the end, but to enjoy the moment. Meditation is the same.

When your mind is really in the present, you have the power do whatever is important for you.

The way to do is to be.

Tao Te Ching

Become aware of your posture. How are you standing or sitting? Being present to what the body is doing is one way to be in this moment.

If when you meditate your mind wanders, notice its wandering, and invite your thoughts to return to the now.

Focus on your gentle breathing, in and out, this moment.

Through it all, we attempt to bring balance to the present moment, understanding that in patience lies wisdom, knowing that what will come next will be determined in large measure by how we are now.

Jon Kabat-Zinn

You don't have to wish you were someplace else, doing something else. You are here, now, doing what you have to do. Relax. Do it. Everything else is superfluous.

Every moment of life is the most exciting, unbelievably miraculous thing you could imagine. Once you appreciate this, then even washing the dishes cannot be despised.

A man who was being chased by a tiger fell over a cliff but clung on to a vine. Just then, two mice began to gnaw through the vine as he hung in mid-air. He spotted a wild strawberry and, on impulse, put it in his mouth. Delicious!

Zen tale

I have realized that the past and future are real illusions, that they exist in the present, which is what there is and all there is.

Alan Watts

You can be the creator of the moment.

Take a moment.

Be in that moment.

Let the moment go.

Let the next moment come.

Living in the moment is living in the breath. Focus on this, and anxiety is soothed.

Every moment is utterly unique and will not be continued in eternity. This fact gives life its poignancy and should concentrate your attention on what you are experiencing now.

Joseph Campbell

Be present, and the past stays where it is. Be present, and the future becomes what it will.

What lies behind us and ahead of us matters not compared to that which is here now.

Are you right here, right now?

Here is your power.

Here is your potential. Take it!

Who you are cannot be defined through thinking or mental labels or definitions, because it's beyond that. It is the very sense of being, or presence, that is there when you become conscious of the present moment.

Eckhart Tolle

Life consists of what you notice.

Let this moment be your teacher.

Today I am living every moment, including the uncomfortable ones.

Breathe in this moment. Place your hand over your diaphragm. Feel it.

The more I notice this moment, the more insight I am granted.

The more I notice this moment, the more power I have to look after myself.

The more I notice this moment, the more care I can offer others.

Walk without a destination. How does it feel, for a moment, not to have a goal other than moving your body and really seeing what you see?

I trust that my body is always in the moment.

My body shows me what is happening right now.

Every moment you are aware of your thoughts adds up to an hour, a day, a week, a month, a year, a lifetime of mindfulness.

When we experience everything the moment has to offer, we better understand our responses—our thoughts, emotions, and physical sensations.

Live each moment completely and the future will take care of itself. Fully enjoy the wonder and beauty of each moment.

Paramahansa Yogananda

The body is always in the present moment. Be fully within your physical body, and you live in the moment.

If we insist on living our lives for the future we stand the danger of ignoring the present.

Let the flow you hold in your hand be your world for that moment.

Don't worry about the future. You are building the future right now.

The Japanese say, "Speak of tomorrow and the devil laughs." The future is never as we imagine, so try not to worry about it.

Look after the
moment, and
you look after
the future.

We can have
hope for the
future, but live
in the now.

There is never a
wrong moment for
a cookie.

You don't need to
design your future;
just accept what's
happening now,
this moment.

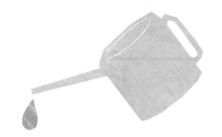

Be here,
be now.

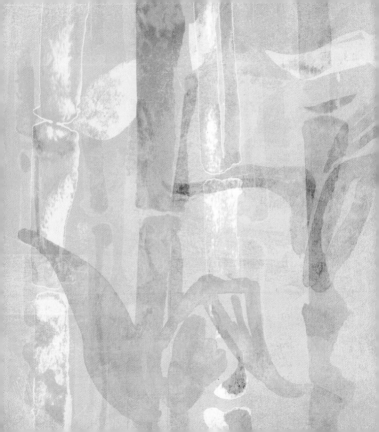

2

Finding peace and calm

Peace begins
with you.

You might be tempted to avoid the messiness of daily living for the tranquility of stillness and peacefulness. This of course would be an attachment to stillness, and like any strong attachment, it leads to delusion. It arrests development and short-circuits the cultivation of wisdom.

Jon Kabat-Zinn

Take time to reflect.
In doing so one
generates many
thoughts and many
ideas.

**A peaceful mind is a
powerful mind.**

There is a proverb that says: the marksman hits the target partly by pulling, partly by letting go. And the boatman reaches dry land partly by pulling, partly by letting go.

Tranquility is one of those things that is harder to find the more frantically you search for it. Relax and let it find you.

Calmness comes through listening. It is impossible to truly listen while doing something else at the same time.

Peace sustains you from the inside.

Often it is possible to experience tranquility by doing and saying nothing at all.

Tranquility is about being natural and being yourself and all that you do.

Much turmoil is created by those who insist on taking you out of yourself while often the tranquility we seek is only found by getting inside ourselves.

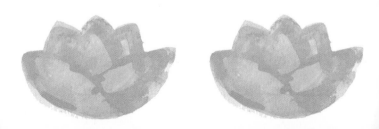

Before you get irritated, take a breath.

Before you judge, put yourself in that person's shoes.

How would they like you to treat them?

We all live in the same hectic world. Some just deal with it better than others.

Learn to value your time alone. When you value something you are keen to protect it.

It is important to realize that peace is less of a destination than a manner of traveling.

Tranquility is often seen far off in the distance when it is right where you are. Only you can grow it.

Peace embraces imaginative reflection rather than judgment. It does not discriminate; no one is chosen, no one is rejected.

People who practice mindfulness still experience stress, and may actually feel emotions more strongly, but they are less likely to be overcome by it and they are likely to recover more quickly.

Anna Black

Serenity does not come as a reward for sacrifice.

The quest for tranquility is not a religious belief. It is for anybody and everybody, and that includes you.

A happy life
consists of
peace of mind.

Walk the internal path
that leads to peace.

Tranquility can be reached
by simply allowing the
mind to become quiet.

The pursuit, even of the best things, ought to be calm and tranquil.

Cicero

Meditation can help us to depart from the general busy activities of the mind to a quiet acceptance of where we are.

Relax your mind and your senses come alive.

Calmness heals much.

Choose to be calm. It is an option.

A calm mind is a healthy mind.

In nature there is no storm that is not followed by calm.

To achieve calm we require patience.

When we can face reality in a calm way then the mind can feel tranquil.

Those who can travel this life calmly unattached and unrepulsed by objects and events can experience true peace.

Cultivate calm in the garden of your heart.

There is more calm to be had from contemplating a day simply spent than from reliving battles.

Discover peace in silence and you will learn that it is possible to journey through the haste and noise of life to placidity.

Let old emotions be gone. Let peace reign in the here and now.

Peace comes after decluttering and organizing our spaces.

Suffer nothing to take away your peace.

Drama is a symptom of poor communication. When you are at peace with yourself, little needs to be said.

Friendship brings peace.

Those who have discovered serenity before us have described it not as being free from the storms, but as finding peace within them.

May I be protected.

May I be peaceful.

May I be well.

May you be protected.

May you be peaceful.

May you be well.

May we all be
protected.

May we all be
peaceful.

May we all be well.

Courage is the price that life exacts for granting peace. The soul that knows it not, knows no release from the little things; knows not the livid loneliness of fear; nor mountain heights where bitter joy can hear the sound of wings.

Amelia Earhart

Peace is not a goal or target; it can occur naturally when activity stops.

Do not squander your contentment by rushing around searching in vain for all the things that cannot bring you peace.

In moments of serenity, we may truly understand the strength of our thoughts.

It is easy to be an angel when no one ruffles your feathers.

Let peace come; don't strive for it.

Patience is a tool of the peacemaker.

You will have peace when you are a part of something peaceful, and that part is within you.

Consider it your duty to increase the peace.

Calm is not a denial of our problems; it allows the formation of creative alternatives for responding to them.

It may be hard to accept with humility that which is offered; it is even harder to accept with serenity that which is denied.

If your mind is as cluttered as an old attic, it is not enough to tidy the room—you must throw things out.

Nothing can bring you peace but yourself.

Ralph Waldo Emerson

Happiness is a matter of being, not having.

I was well into middle age before it struck me that there was absolutely nothing to prevent me from being as happy as I wanted.

True strength is deep calm.

Whatever you say about living a happy and peaceful life can sound like a motto from some tacky souvenir. This doesn't devalue happiness; it just demonstrates how widely the idea has caught on.

Generals can win by force of arms, but Gandhi defied an empire using nothing but peaceful resistance.

When you love outwardly, you express peace inwardly.

When you realize that the tranquility is within you, your relationships flourish.

When you trust yourself completely, you can know peace more deeply.

When you remove ego and desire from your friendship, you and your friend will be left with peace.

When the power of love overcomes the love of power, the world will know peace.

Jimi Hendrix

In stillness we
may find the map
that shows the
way to our power.

Peace is not
the absence of
conflict, but the
true strength of a
courageous heart.

Our greatest joy lies in building a peaceful relationship with ourselves.

Be at peace with who you are now; don't struggle. You are not who you think you should be, or who you thought you were.

101

Where there is chaos may you
not be chaotic.

Where there is strife may you
be still.

Where there is **darkness may**
your peaceful light **shine.**

Sit quietly doing nothing.
Spring comes and the **grass**
grows.

When we are at peace with the person we truly are, we give others permission to accept themselves. We do not reject our imperfections or theirs.

Be conscious, be now, be calm.

Rather than connecting to nature's simplicity, we opt for an excited mind.

Kiva Bottero

Peace is not the avoidance of trouble; rather, it is the calm resilience that comes with being brave and looking conflict right in the eye.

Wherever I am now is the place of serenity within.

When those around you fight, be still. This too will pass.

Focus on your gentle breathing. It does it all by itself. There is nothing else to do.

Just Don't Worry

Take strides to make friends with yourself—you will not only let go of an enemy, but find the best friend you can ever have.

In the bright eyes of someone else's friendship we can see the reflection of our own, and in serenity know that we give a precious gift.

Friendship is an understanding between two people, which brings them both peace.

Peace begins with a smile.

Mother Teresa

Don't worry. These are just your thoughts.

Be with what's good today. Feel calm just appreciating what's right with you, not what's wrong.

Be still, and listen. Can you hear a sound without giving it meaning?

Take a small task and experience it to the full. Notice even the smallest actions you take as you eat, shower, make a drink. Make these tasks your daily meditations.

In quiet spaces the mind is quiet.

When the words of your enemies are ringing in your head, find peace by meditating on the silence of your friend.

When you do not feed anger or jealousy with attention, there can be no anger or jealousy—only calm.

You don't need to make things
all right.

You don't need anything to be
perfect.

You don't need to rehearse the
future.

You need only to be here in peace.

May peace be with you.

3
Minding our thoughts

Most of us take for granted
that time flies, meaning that
it passes too quickly. But in
the mindful state, time doesn't
really pass at all. There is only
a single instant of time that
keeps renewing itself over and
over with infinite variety.

Deepak Chopra

Your thoughts affect the physiology of your brain and the physiology affects your thoughts.

Ruby Wax

Life boils down to what you say yes to and what you say no to.

John C Parkin

If you change the way you look at things, the things you look at change.

Wayne Dyer

Just for today, try to let go of your expectations. Be with who and where you are, right now.

Enjoy the feeling of just being.

I am enough.

You are enough.

We are enough.

We can all be mindful of
our thoughts.

Adjust your mindset.

Change your thoughts, change your reality.

I used to think that the brain was the most wonderful organ in my body. Then I realized who was telling me this.

Emo Philips

Notice when you're mindless—judging others. Notice when you're mindless—judging yourself. Then congratulate yourself on this noticing.

When you accept everything as acceptable, you accept yourself.

You might feel you know your mind, but do you know your heart as well?

Our thoughts create our reality. What do you think?

Love is a butterfly, which when pursued is just beyond your grasp, but if you will sit down quietly it may alight upon you.

Nathaniel Hawthorne

Once you start counting your blessings, it may be hard to stop.

Meditation trains the mind the way physical exercise strengthens the body.

Sharon Salzberg

Higher levels of understanding will come naturally from the positive feelings that surface when judgmental thoughts about separate realities are dismissed.

121

What do you pay
attention to?

What do you give
meaning to?

How different from
yesterday could today be?

Learn to understand
instead of immediately
judging.

Listen without prejudice.

If we look into our own minds, we can see that the unhealthy aspects of ourselves often show up in our contact with others. When we find problems with another person, we only see the gross extensions of their personality. It's easy to forget that we are concentrating on just one or two aspects of them. We then use these impressions to support a fixed and hostile view.

Christopher Titmuss

So much of the time spent in our lives is the product of imagined ideas about how some other person thinks or feels.

For today, focus on only what is happening now. Do not entertain negative words, thoughts, or actions, even small thoughts.

Change never stops changing.

Why worry about the future? It just came and went.

You have free will to make new choices each and every day.

It is not primarily our physical selves that limit us but rather our mindset about our physical limits.

Ellen J Langer

People think they have a little mind in their head and a big one that knows the world outside. These two are the same—they just have different names.

Are you what you think?

To a mind that is still, the whole universe surrenders.

Chuang-Tzu

The city of the self is in the state of mind.

Certain thoughts are prayers. There are moments when, whatever the attitude of the body, the soul is on its knees.

Victor Hugo

It is the mark of an educated mind to be able to entertain a thought without accepting it.

Aristotle

Reading furnishes the mind only with materials of knowledge; it is thinking that makes what we read ours.

John Locke

Your noticing the world changes the world in some unseen way.

Choose carefully what you pay attention to and what you ignore, both inside yourself and in the world. These things make up your life.

Be the silent watcher of your thoughts and behavior. You are beneath the thinker. You are the stillness beneath the mental noise. You are the love and joy beneath the pain.

Eckhart Tolle

Be still in a forest. Allow your thoughts to be the only movement in the stillness. Your mind is your power in silence. Listen with your spirit.

While man complicates his life, every other creature is busy enjoying it.

Think big thoughts. Relish small pleasures.

When you ask others what they think, be prepared to listen with full attention.

If I don't agree with you, it is not because I have not been listening.

You can train your attention to be attentive. When your thoughts stray from the present, simply invite your attention to return like a friend walking back through the door into your house.

Look at your mind. Watch the thoughts rise and fall. See how they come and go and never stay in one place for long. What creature is this with such a fluttering candle flame for a mind?

A mature mind does not crave certainty.

The real training of the mind is not done in school. It is accomplished by learning to observe our thoughts, then letting them go as we choose.

When you give someone a piece of your mind, it is the right piece?

Everyone is attracted to a kind and generous mind.

Meditation is both exercise and nourishment for the mind. It will repay the time you invest in it many times over.

You are pretty enlightened if you realize you have to keep your brain in shape.

Ruby Wax

Minds affect one another.
Let yours enjoy the
influence of people whose
minds can benefit yours.

Bright minds
cast their
light on one
another.

Do not accept any limit to your potential. The human mind is the most remarkable and complex construction we know. We have hardly begun to understand all that it can do.

Mind always matters.

Everything you can imagine
is real.

Pablo Picasso

Imagination is the magic carpet of the mind.

Our thought is limitless. It can take us to unknown worlds, indeed right to the ends of the universe.

You wouldn't fill your house with garbage. Treat your mind with the same care.

Be the observer of your thoughts. Like fallen leaves, they come, they go.

Curiosity is the means by which we humans constantly develop the mind.

Learn to trust that part of the mind that you can't see.

The subtle parts of your mind will speak to you if you keep quiet long enough to let them.

Problems exist in the mind, and it is within the power of the mind to embrace and observe them.

The best mind-altering drug is truth.

Welcome your sad thoughts with gentleness, then when it is time, let them go.

Every great discovery, every revolution in thought, started life as a passing notion in someone's mind.

The discovery that the mind can regulate its thoughts, fostering some and dismissing others, is one of the most important stages in the art of self-culture.

John Cowper Powys

A mind made up doesn't signify that thinking is finished.

However compassionate we are, we can never see entirely into the mind of another.

Acceptance dwells nowhere but in the mind.

Bless your body always. Speak no word of condemnation about it.

How extraordinary that we let bad hair ruin a whole day.

Your body is where you live.

Think with the whole of yourself—body and mind working together.

The physical is not second best to the spiritual; the two are different aspects of the same thing.

Feel gratitude for all your body does for you.

Your body has its own wisdom, and gives you messages through your senses. Are you listening?

Pay attention to yourself. If you weed your yard, have your car serviced, and repaint your house, why neglect your body?

Your body is naturally present in this moment. Exercise and movement help your mind join your body in the moment, too.

Exercise for the body is medicine for the mind.

For some, the life of the mind is an alternative to the life of the body. To the wise, they are one and the same.

Your body is thinking. What are its thoughts? Comfort, discomfort, an ache, an itch?

Take a mindful walk each day and absorb just what you see and sense—nothing more, nothing less.

Age is an issue of mind over matter. If you don't mind, it doesn't matter.

Mark Twain

Man holds an inward talk with his self alone, which it behooves him to regulate well.

Blaise Pascal

Ask yourself: how important is it?

Are you really your thoughts?

It's not what happens to you, but how you react to it that matters.

Epictetus

Life flows with you
if you think it does.

If you ever find
yourself in the wrong
story, leave.

Mo Willems

Destroy your "to-do" list. Think in the now.

According to science, the bumblebee should never get off the ground. It must be his strong belief that gets him airborne.

Trust your intuitive thoughts. Don't beat them into submission; when you do this, they will just come back for attention.

What you see depends on what you see, not always what you look for.

Your feelings are just feelings; your thoughts, just thoughts.

Tomorrow can take care of itself.

Nature gives us so much—be thankful.

Practice an attitude of gratitude.

I am grateful for what I am
and have. My thanksgiving
is perpetual. It is surprising
how contented one can be with
nothing definite—only a sense of
existence. My breath is sweet to
me. O how I laugh when I think
of my vague indefinite riches.
No run on my bank can drain it,
for my wealth is not possession
but enjoyment.

Henry David Thoreau

Gratitude increases abundance; poverty-consciousness creates lack.

Friendship is something we offer even when those we offer it to are unable to acknowledge our help or show any gratitude.

Show gratitude for everything.

I am open to what this moment brings.

I do not judge.

I feel what I feel, I think what I think.

Each moment, I like myself even more.

Each night before you sleep, be thankful for three or more things in your life—whatever kind of day you have had, there is always something to be thankful for.

Happy the heart that keeps its
twilight hour,
And, in the depths of heavenly
peace reclined,
Loves to commune with
thoughts of tender power—
Thoughts that ascend, like
angels beautiful,
A shining Jacob's-ladder of
the mind!

Paul Hamilton Hayne

The thoughts you choose define your state of mind.

May our thoughts
set us free.

I am limitless in
my thinking.

4
Facing fears

Mindfulness does not erase negative memories; it "transcends" them, giving us back our deepest power which resides in our hearts.

Christopher Dines

When we change, all life changes.

Why conform? One comes
into this life free and equal
so why throw this to the wind
by spending one's life trying
to create a life that is just like
everyone else's?

Tranquility comes when we can
accept ourselves for who we
truly are, in the present, not the
past or the future.

Don't feel guilty about making things easy for yourself.

Sit and be calm. When you see a bird in flight, allow your eyes to fly with it. Admire it. Taste the day.

Do not fear to open the doors that lie between what is known and what is unknown.

Do nothing and be brave about it.

Never underestimate yourself for the world will insist on taking you at face value.

Nature is infinitely patient, infinitely calm. Everything comes, everything passes.

The past cannot be changed by you and worrying about the future will only serve to ruin your present.

Why spend your life worrying about the future? You will know when it comes.

You do not need to constantly compare your happiness with that of others. Contentment denies comparison.

The world is filled with people waiting for some miracle to improve the state of things. Yet while they wait, their own responsibilities are neglected.

We're all of us merely passers-by.

You will discover that there will be good days and bad days for you, for me, and for everyone else. You're never alone.

In life we are many things. Be receptive to the glorious uncertainty of living.

Be in harmony with nature. Nature does not assess fear and without fear the heart may be quiet.

It is impossible to separate yourself from the universe. You are one and the same.

Try being as an infant knowing nothing except what you hear, see, smile at, and feel.

We may learn fear when we are children, but as adults we can unlearn it.

Take time to observe water in all the forms it takes: rain droplets, trickles, spray, waves, and torrents.

Observe cats and how they can sit for hours and just watch. They are not stressed, they do not panic.

Accept the necessity for suffering and the value of suffering.

Step out of your usual perspective on your life and new possibilities will open up.

Learn to accept that you are not perfect—nobody is.

You will discover
that whatever you
thought before,
you are a child of
the universe and,
like the stars in
the sky and the
trees in the park,
you have a right
to be here.

It is okay to feel angry.

Respect your weaknesses and make the most of your strengths.

It is good to laugh often.

Allow yourself some quiet time for meditation.

The beginning of losing one's misery comes through the resolution to get to know oneself. Then you may begin to create room in your life for other things and people who will bring you joy.

Feeling you should be happy when everything inside you is telling you to be unhappy is like trying to correct nature— be unhappy and patient, and happiness will come.

If you can forgive yourself for the mistakes you make, you will find true happiness.

It may sound strange, but it is possible to be happy about the fact that you are unhappy.

I am enough just the way I am now.

Do not let fear stop you.

Unhappiness is a season that will pass, bringing sunshine and flowers.

We may feel fear, but in reality we are okay—after all, we are here.

Imagine getting past the point of fear and saying, "I stared at fear fully in the face and got through it, and I'm ready to take anything else that life has to throw at me!"

Live your life according to the light that is within you.

Because you are capable of enjoying life, you cannot fail at anything.

The best medicines in life can be found in a faithful friend or a happy moment.

Don't worry about your entire future—it can only arrive one day at a time.

Trust in yourself.

Don't burden yourself with anger for your enemies. Forgive them. That will make them really angry!

Be your own best friend when you're happy and unhappy.

A halo doesn't go with everything and is just something else to worry about losing.

Think of your
problems as a
challenge in a
game you enjoy
playing.

Your confidence
can make others
less afraid.

If you suffer from feelings of helplessness or frustration, walk in nature.

If you doubt yourself and feel stuck, walk in nature.

If you feel alone, walk in nature.

In nature you will see that every season has its place, and each one is beautiful.

Who says that you can't live the life you dream?

It is easy to feel isolated in personal sadness, but remember, no sorrow is new.

Your joy is your sorrow
unmasked and the
selfsame well from which
your laughter rises was
oftentimes filled with
your tears.

Kahlil Gibran

Effective communication is essential to a happy life. Feel free to talk about positive feelings of love, joy, and appreciation as well as negative feelings of anger, fear, and disappointment.

To live well requires the exercise of practical wisdom—moderation, justice, and courage—to balance pleasures against pains and to accept, when necessary, those pains that lead to greater pleasures.

Pure and complete sorrow is as impossible as pure and complete joy.

Leo Tolstoy

Weeping may endure for a night, but joy cometh in the morning.

Psalms 30:5

Democritus, known as the "Laughing Philosopher", proposed happiness, or "cheerfulness," as the highest good—a condition to be achieved through moderation, tranquility, and freedom from fear.

The lies that are allowed to sink in do the most hurt.

To everything there is a season.

You can try to get to the root of any unhappiness by interpreting your dreams. The explanations of the experts always give you something to laugh at.

Each new day has a past, present, and future. There, you see? Things have already moved on.

One step at a time.
And so the most
arduous journey is
completed.

Climb to the top of the
boulder that blocks
your way, and enjoy the
view from a different
perspective.

Consider the things that make you ill at ease, and they will begin to lose their power.

Consider the things that bring you happiness, and more of these will enter your life.

Life is a cycle of destruction and healing. The wisest of us are patient whatever the situation and happy in the knowledge that healing or calm will follow.

Does your happiness depend upon internal or external things—or both?

There are no obstacles in life—only stepping stones of all shapes and sizes.

It's only thinking, so don't give it another thought.

The wise heart is often one that has been broken.

When the heart weeps for what is lost, the spirit laughs for what it has found.

Sufi saying

When we have a sense of humor we can feel comfortable about anything that life throws at us.

Everything you need to be you, you already have.

A defeat is only a minor, temporary setback.

Let wonder replace fear.

I like living. I have sometimes been wildly, despairingly, acutely miserable, wracked with sorrow, but through it all I still know quite certainly that just to be alive is a grand thing.

Agatha Christie

It's possible to be content with who you are.

We cannot be made uncomfortable without our approval.

Sometimes the obstacle we must overcome is the path itself.

Worry is more
exhausting
than running a
marathon.

You will not defeat
tomorrow's difficulties by
worrying; you will only
serve to drain today of its
strength.

Difficult times have helped me to understand better than before, how infinitely rich and beautiful life is in every way, and that so many things that one goes worrying about are of no importance whatsoever.

Isak Dinesen

The way to overcome great problems or obstacles is to start immediately, by doing all the small things you make your mind up to do, no matter how much you don't want to do them right now.

We close our eyes to the world and cry out that it is dark. We open our eyes to the world and see so much that cannot be named in a word.

Many a dream has been silenced by security.

I will not live in the continual fear that I might make a mistake.

I do not fear being wrong. That is what gives me my confidence.

When we choose to liberate ourselves from fear, we set a pattern for many others in our circle of friends and associates to follow.

The moment we can do what we fear, our fear disappears.

Nobody is comfortable about doing something courageous. You have to be frightened before you can show courage.

When someone offers you abuse, politely refuse to accept it and reply, "Now it belongs to you."

Having an even temper means never having to get even.

Every opportunity to develop anger presents the same opportunity to develop patience.

By all means write down your angry words, but you don't have to send them.

Why be angry? The moment has already passed.

When we feel resentment it is not relevant to the present moment; it is reacting to past pain.

Our real blessings often appear to us in the shape of pains, losses, and disappointments; but let us have patience and we soon shall see them in their proper figures.

Joseph Addison

Plants need rain
to grow and so
do people.

A rock may change the river's course, but it does not change the river.

If people won't meet you half way, keep walking towards them; that way you will reach them even if they refuse to move; then you can invite them to walk alongside you.

The obstacle is the path.

Zen saying

Don't worry about problems. Jumping over hurdles just makes you fitter.

If I am perfect, I have no cracks —so how will I be happy if the sun can't get in?

I have everything
I need right here
within me. I am
perfect exactly as
I am.

Judy Hall

If you're reading these words, perhaps it's because something has kicked open the door for you, and you're ready to embrace change. It isn't enough to appreciate change from afar, or only in the abstract, or as something that can happen to other people but not to you. We need to create change for ourselves, in a workable way, as part of our everyday lives.

Sharon Salzberg

If we choose to remain
as we are, fearing that
change is painful, we live
with fear.

If we choose to embrace
change and its pain, we
grow, and live without fear.

Don't fear fear.

We talk of "embracing change" for a reason—it comes as a lover, not as an enemy.

When people shake their heads because we are living in a restless age, ask them how they would like to live in a stationary one and do without change.

George Bernard Shaw

Getting older is not really a problem—it's the idea of getting older that causes trouble.

My mother says she didn't mind her 70s but hates her 80s. To my certain knowledge, she said the same about every previous decade. Maybe they're all okay in the end.

Be gentle with yourself and others when making changes. Let nothing be forced.

Dying is our greatest change and everyone fears it. But what would a world without death look like? If there was no winter, how could we have the spring?

"Everything flows," Heraclitus said. "You can't step into the same river twice." And remember, it isn't only the river that changes.

This moment is unique, and however you experience it, it will not return again the same.

People fear change the way they fear the unseen monster in a ghost story. Once you see it, then it's just a guy in a rubber suit.

Life is wiggly like live eels in a bucket. They move constantly because that is the nature of eels.

God, grant me the serenity to accept the things I cannot change, the courage to change the things I can, and the wisdom to know the difference.

In Britain they say, "If you don't like our weather, wait a minute." Life's the same; if you don't like what's happening, don't worry. It will soon change.

Change is the only evidence of life.

Evelyn Waugh

If one changes internally, one should not continue to live with the same objects. This reflects one's mind and psyche of yesterday. I throw away what has no dynamic living use.

Anaïs Nin

Change is exciting—like going on a long journey without taking a map.

I have examined myself thoroughly and come to the conclusion that I don't need to change much.

Sigmund Freud

You're not a thing, you're a process. Just as an eddy in a stream is constantly changing, so are you. Is staying the same an option?

We need times when we separate ourselves from family and friends and go to new places. It is only by being without what is familiar that we can be open to change.

People like to do things the same way they've always done them because it saves the trouble of thinking.

Change used to be valued for its results, but nowadays it is often seen as a good thing in itself.

Always! That is a dreadful word... it is a meaningless word, too.

Oscar Wilde

However much you change, you will always still be you and therefore, in your own eyes, very much the same.

I look back at my younger self with horror. On the other hand, at least she had enough sense to change into me.

Full fathom five thy father lies;
Of his bones are coral made;
Those are pearls that were
     his eyes:
Nothing of him that doth fade,
But doth suffer a sea-change
Into something rich and strange.

Shakespeare, The Tempest

Not all change has to be useful. You don't have to repaint the house just to protect the wood, you do it because you want a new color. It is enough that some change is just for fun.

Just as we outgrow favorite clothes, we may also outgrow friends, colleagues, jobs, hobbies—sometimes while they're still in good condition and before we've found replacements.

A friend resigned from his job and I asked him why. He said, "Sometimes you just have to leave, even if you don't know where you're going."

There's a time for some changes. Why you can give up smoking or go on a diet successfully one day and not on others is a mystery. Knowing how to pick the right moment is an art worth cultivating.

Young people sometimes look ahead and say, "I'll never be able to cope with what the future holds." Not so. The person you are now might not be able to, but the person you're becoming will.

Vulnerability
in the face
of constant
change is
what we share,
whatever
our present
condition.

Sharon Salzberg

Do not be disconcerted by joy, even though it seems a little excessive in our troubled times. The Chinese have a proverb that says a single joy scatters a hundred griefs.

The world is embarrassed by simplicity and goodness and therefore hides in cleverness and complexity. Fortunately, simplicity and goodness won't go away.

Sometimes all you
can do is laugh.
If you can laugh,
you're not sunk yet.

Your life may not be perfect but
as long as it's what you want
and not what someone else
thinks you ought to want, you'll
be happy.

Every drop of rain makes
the river stronger.

It's okay to be miserable.

It's okay to be happy.

Seek not happiness too greedily,
and be not fearful of unhappiness.

Tao Te Ching

You are full of potential miracles. The risk is worth it.

A friend, no longer in the first flush of youth, volunteered for a charity parachute jump. "How will you do it?" everyone asked her. "Easy, there's only one way down and you don't need a road map."

People will love
you in spite of your
mistakes.

People will love you
because of your
mistakes.

When you make a choice, you change the future.

Deepak Chopra

Sometimes you can quell anger in others by listening to what they have to say.

When we are in emotional pain, it can be better to pay attention to it than run from it. Pain just wants to be noticed.

Grief is a friend. It
serves to remind us,
It makes us take action,
It is our teacher,
And our foothold back
to joy.

In the depths of winter, I
finally learnt in me there
was an invincible summer.

Albert Camus

5

Loving kindness and self-compassion

When we have genuine self-love, we can tap into our true goodness, see the gifts we have been given and then experience the joy of sharing them with others.

Dr Patrizia Collard

Wherever you go, go with all your heart.

Confucius

Compassion fills the heart.

Listen to others no matter how dull they seem, for everyone has their story.

Take time to discover the best in others.

When you listen to somebody attentively you listen not only to the words, but also to the feeling of what it is being conveyed—to the whole of it, not part of it.

Don't forget to love yourself.

Søren Kierkegaard

If you set about doing something put your heart into it and enjoy it that way regardless of the outcome; it will be a positive experience.

Do not try to be all things to everyone. Be content to be yourself to yourself.

Take time to love—it is the most powerful medicine on earth.

True compassion is the swiftest path to tranquility.

Anything will give up
its secrets if you love it
enough.

Not only have I found that when
I talk to the little flower or to the
little peanut they will give up their
secrets, but I have found that when I
silently commune with people they
give up their secrets also—if you
love them enough.

George Washington Carver

What does love look like? It has the hands to help others. It has the feet to hasten to the poor and needy. It has eyes to see misery and want. It has the ears to hear the sighs and sorrows of men. That is what love looks like.

Saint Augustine

He who is in love
is wise and is
becoming wiser,
sees newly every
time he looks at
the object beloved,
drawing from it
with his eyes and
his mind those
virtues it possesses.

Ralph Waldo Emerson

Love is patient and kind; love is not jealous or boastful; it is not arrogant or rude.

I Corinthians: 13

Love is as simple and as difficult as this: love one another and you will be happy.

Love is found in the most unexpected places.

Anyone who plants trees loves others besides himself.

Be yourself. That is the quickest route to love.

You don't just feel love, you do love, act love, live love.

Love is shelter; come in from the rain.

Love is about letting people be themselves.

Open your heart and be prepared to give, and love will find you.

The snow goose need not bathe to make itself white. Neither need you do anything but be yourself.

When we stop judging and start appreciating people's differences, we begin to learn from them.

You must listen
to your own
heart, which will
never lie to you.

Cherish the music that
stays in your heart.

Nobody can be
exactly like you; learn
to accept and love
your uniqueness.

No matter who you are and how confused you are about life, there is one prayer that will provide the key to your tranquility and that is simply to say thank you.

If you want to give love, first love yourself.

We are all capable
of loving and of
being loved.

Love is wanting what
we have, not what we
can't have.

Love grows
by giving.

A spouse is someone who knows the song in your heart and can sing it back to you when you forget the words.

Love is having someone who accepts you just the way you are today.

Love is, above all,
the gift of oneself.

The heart is a garden
where love grows wild.

We live where
we love.

Everyone becomes a poet when they are touched by love.

The most profound relationship any of us will have in this life is the one we have with ourselves.

No amount of self-improvement can make up for any lack of self-acceptance.

Robert Holden

Love is the expression of simplicity in emotion.

Luyen Dao

To love is to be vulnerable.

C S Lewis

Love is something eternal;
the aspect may change,
but not the essence.

Vincent van Gogh

Spread love everywhere you go;
first of all in your own home.
Give love to your children, to a
wife or husband, to a next-door
neighbor.

Mother Teresa

Kindness in words creates confidence,
Kindness in thinking creates profoundness,
Kindness in giving creates love.

Lao Tzu

Mindfulness without kindness is not mindfulness.

Anna Black

The best portion of a good man's life is his little, nameless, unremembered acts of kindness and of love.

William Wordsworth

I celebrate myself, and sing myself.

Walt Whitman

The longest relationship you're going to have in this life is with yourself, so you make certain that you like yourself.

We make a living by what we get,
but we make a life by what we give.

Winston Churchill

Loving kindness toward the self
is the ultimate path to healing
ourselves. When we become
whole through self-love, we can
truly show love and compassion
toward others.

No one can be you better
than you.

We keep passing unseen through little moments of other people's lives.

Robert M Pirsig

Do not be afraid of showing your affection. Be warm and tender, thoughtful, and affectionate. Men are more helped by sympathy, than by service; love is more than money, and a kind word will give more pleasure than a present.

Sir John Lubbock

Love thrives on generosity.

The gardener who was happy to plant the tree that he would never see grown has provided the shade for our comfort.

Bloom where you are planted.

Take the thing you least like about yourself and generate a feeling of compassion towards this part of you. Practice loving what you don't like, and you can begin to love it.

We are so often caught up in our destination that we forget to appreciate the journey, especially the kindness of the people we meet on our path. Appreciation is a wonderful feeling, don't overlook it.

We are all as one.

Be good.
Be kind.
Be humane.
Be charitable.
Console the afflicted.

Truth is generally kindness,
but where the two diverge
and collide, kindness should
override truth.

Samuel Butler

The wonderful thing about human beings is that we each possess the ability to turn someone else's life around for the better.

Learn to share your love with others, but keep part of this love for yourself.

Paulo Coelho

A heart can never be too full.

Kindness often removes difficulty.

Where there is hatred, there is a path to love.

Charity begins in the heart.

Make love, not paperwork.

Ask yourself, what would Love do now?

Loving yourself isn't selfish. It's a measure of how much you can love others.

We can love others only as much as we love ourselves.

Lorna Byrne

Compassion includes you.

Self-compassion grows from a bud into the flower of compassion for others.

Kindness is wisdom.
There is none in life
But needs it and may
learn.

Philip James Bailey

Kindness is
produced by
kindness.

Cicero

No act of kindness, however small, is ever wasted.

Aesop

Kindness is doubled when we give willingly, with all our hearts.

Find comfort in who you are.

There are some among us
on this earth who manage
to leave everything a little
better than it was before.

Tell others how wonderful
you think they are.

Welcome the outstretched
hand.

Whenever a compassionate person listens to your troubles, do not think that this listener has had no troubles of their own. Because of their pain they are able to offer the balm of their presence.

When you look beyond the imperfections, everyone is perfect.

We are all part of one another, and all involved in one another.

Imagine the very best friend a person could ever have.

First, become that friend to yourself.

Then become that friend to someone else in your life.

My best friend is not only my best friend—my best friend is my second self.

See if you can give yourself gifts that may be true blessings, such as self-acceptance, or some time each day with no purpose. Practice feeling deserving enough to accept these gifts without obligation—to simply receive from yourself, and from the universe.

Jon Kabat-Zinn

Fill someone's life with sweetness.

Share a little of what you are good at doing.

A single candle can light many others; so it is with happiness and people.

Sow courtesy.
Reap friendship.
Plant kindness.
Harvest love.

When we do things in the spirit of friendship or the spirit of love, at those moments we are truly alive.

Be tender with the young—for we are all young sometime.

Be compassionate with the aged—for we are all aged sometime.

Have sympathy for those who suffer— for we all suffer sometimes.

Just because an animal is large, it doesn't mean he doesn't want kindness; however big Tigger seems to be, remember that he wants as much kindness as Roo.

A A Milne

If you want happiness for an hour—take a nap.
If you want happiness for a day—go fishing.
If you want happiness for a month—get married.
If you want happiness for a year—inherit a fortune.
If you want happiness for a lifetime—help others.

Chinese proverb

The hardest forms of compassion are for people you don't love.

Paul Gilbert

Moderation in all things—except love.

The greatest gift we can give to another is our undivided attention.

Pave your path to emotional growth with good humor and compassion.

When we show compassion, it easier for others to like and accept themselves.

All deeds of kindness and beneficence take root in the soil of the patient heart.

Next time you say, "How are you?" see what happens when you are genuinely interested in the answer.

We are here on earth to do good for others. What the others are here for, I don't know.

W H Auden

A good talker is a companion but a good listener is gold.

A kind word is like a spring day.

Russian proverb

Give a flower and the scent lingers on your fingers.

Chinese proverb

Forget injuries,
never forget
kindnesses.

Confucius

The bees know that the
farmer who wants a
healthy crop always helps
his poorer neighbor out
with good seed.

If the only prayer
you ever say in
your entire life is
thank you, it will be
enough.

Meister Eckhart

Have you ever seen the expression on the face of a traffic warden when you feed a stranger's expired meter?

Life sends you good things whether you are grateful or not. But with gratitude, life sends them to you faster. That is because gratitude is a state of being.

Neale Donald Walsch

I refuse to accept the view that mankind is so tragically bound to the starless midnight of racism and war that the bright daybreak of peace and brotherhood can never become a reality... I believe that unarmed truth and unconditional love will have the final word.

Martin Luther King Jr

6

Creativity and success

Be patiently alert to the creativity of each moment and be aware of what takes place in or outside yourself.

Creative genius has the faculty of perceiving in a non-habitual way.

Inside each of us is a child who still wants to play—this is our creative desire.

Try this: look, now see what it is you are looking at. Notice this in every detail, appreciate every nuance. This is mindfulness, this is creative engagement.

An altered state of consciousness marks the birth of a new idea.

Never underestimate the immense therapeutic value of becoming involved in creative pursuits.

Seek out methods of expanding your mind—this has a remarkable way of accelerating your creative potential.

Nothing can bring mankind closer in common to the creation of the universe than his own acts of creativity.

Creativity is always exploring its environment. One should always seek to exercise one's imagination and never be limited to the extent of our backyard—this is what separates the adult imagination from children's. We are mature enough to go out beyond the garden gate and play.

In order to create well, one must first become good at thinking well.

We learn because it is in our very nature to do so. To grow, thrive, develop, and progress are things that humans do, given even the slimmest of opportunities.

Get creative: go back to nature for information.

Converse with nature and it will provide inspiration to those who seek it.

Forget success or failure and just get on with being creative.

Life is an ongoing creative adventure. Whatever our expectations, everything can change at the drop of a hat, so remain flexible.

One can wait forever for a creative muse to arrive or better, develop a knack of getting in touch with one's own inner child.

One must take up arms to defeat habit; this is how originality wins through.

One cannot live a creative life without first letting go of the fear of being wrong.

What is the value of a single idea? Each is an acorn capable of producing a thousand forests.

We are all creative: life itself is an art.

The creative view is that the world owes you nothing, and everything is a gift.

Every day there exist hundreds of possibilities to work at doing things more creatively.

When there is care, there is creativity.

Look around you for creative materials. Old tickets, magazines, and fabric—whatever is around you now is good enough to begin with. See these items anew. Give them another name.

Our creativity helps us to clear our minds and create more balance in our lives.

Our muses urge us to try to be mindful and to let things take their natural course.

No matter how attuned we may become to our surroundings and the world around us, each time we embark upon a creative journey that takes us into our inner world we will always discover new territory.

All creativity is based upon our most fundamental human need, which is to know oneself deeply and in relation to the rest of the world.

The greatest creative discovery any of us can make is that we can all alter our lives by altering our state of mind.

Wherever we may look, we will be able to find that which nourishes us, inspires us, and deepens our creative experience.

Creativity, whether in a group, an individual exercise, or a multinational project—from arranging a vase filled with flowers to coordinating a global experience—comes down to two key words: meaningful interaction.

Sometimes the most creative thing we can do is to simplify the overcomplicated.

Ponder this: each day we grow happy in the knowledge that we do not know where our creative limits lie.

Every creative day is the portal of new revelations and new discovery.

The essence of creativity is coming to terms with the "me" that we each are, of taking comfort from the things that "me" can do, and developing the confidence and skills to do the things that "me" would like to do.

There are as many inspirations to be had in the bathtub as there are in a cathedral.

A change in perspective brings a whole new world of opportunity.

Show me an unhappy gardener.

Who can be uninspired in a garden?

Time spent in creative activities such as music, art, hobbies, education, and community service is more conducive to happiness than passive recreations such as television, radio, and spectator sports.

A tree trunk the size of a man
grows from a blade as thin as a
hair.
A tower nine stories high is built
from a small heap of earth.
A journey of a thousand miles
starts in front of your feet.

Lao Tzu

Try writing... a list,
a letter, a journal, a
novel, a declaration.

Are we able to free up all our creative energy to generate a peaceful and happy existence?

An act of creativity is an act of integrity.

Every living person has creative potential: we are constantly discovering ourselves.

Be aware of what you do well and use this to bring you success; play to your strengths, and let your weaknesses lend you wisdom.

When men are easy in their circumstances, they are naturally enemies to innovations.

Joseph Addison

If you can grow in self-awareness and stay alert, positive, and open, when a unique opportunity presents itself you will recognize its potential—and have the reserves of energy to take action.

Don't give up on your dreams. With passion and attention, you can't go wrong.

A musician must make music, an artist must paint, a poet must write; and to do so, they will be patient with themselves.

Don't follow the
path; clear a
new one.

Trust and accept that
things will work out
in the end.

When you are truly ready for a thing, it usually shows up.

Don't worry about the future. Focus on accomplishing what's right in front of you right now.

When we are completely immersed in our project, time appears not to exist at all.

Be part of the serene creative process going on all around you in nature.

Think of yourself as a creative person. Decide that your ideas are of value.

The creative spirit lurks silently deep within us. You won't find it by looking, but then again you won't find it by not looking. The strange thing is that if you allow yourself to be truly receptive, your creativity will find you.

Carry your success lightly.

Cooking is one of the few forms of creativity that provides immense and immediate satisfaction both to yourself and those you share it with.

We can all be creative when we cook.

Make the preparation of every meal a sensory experience. Smell, taste, touch, and observe each ingredient as a precious gift.

The best place to practice self-expression is in the kitchen through your cooking.

Sometimes it feels better to bake bread and enjoy a good loaf than to travel five thousand miles in search of a beach.

Writers write. Musicians play. Artists make art. Teachers teach. Always remember what you do, and do it.

Whatever you create, do it with your heart.

The best communication is intended to inform the recipient, not make the writer look clever.

Read over your compositions, and wherever you find a passage which you think is particularly fine, strike it out.

Samuel Johnson

If your success does not help you grow as a person, does not open your mind to new insights and new aspirations, then it is a poor thing.

What are the secrets of your success?

I want to do it because I want to do it.

Amelia Earhart

My mother said, "If you become a soldier you'll end up as a general and if you become a monk you'll end up as the Pope." Instead I became a painter and ended up as Picasso.

Pablo Picasso

In World War I, the troops would sing, "We're here because we're here because we're here because we're here." Sometimes that's all the motivation you need.

A clever idea isn't clever because it's hard for others to understand; it's clever because of its simplicity and because no one else noticed it before.

Work at your own pace and your strength will never leave you. Knowing the rhythms of your body will make you ten times stronger.

Even governments only tax
people according to their means.

Give yourself time
for movement and
rest alongside your
work. Be gentle
with yourself.

All people have within them
seeds of immense greatness.
All you need do is water them
regularly.

The way you run
your life is your
biggest creation.

Failure is a unique method of being granted another chance to get it right.

Success can sometimes spring from failure. Don't reject your mistakes, embrace them.

No amount of worldly success will ever compensate for the lack of a quiet, contented mind.

The secret of success in life is for a man to be ready for his opportunity when it comes.

Benjamin Disraeli

Be content to view the success of others for what it is and not as a negative comment on your own life.

Include the success of others in your dreams for your own success.

Success is liking yourself, liking what you do, and liking how you do it.

Maya Angelou

Simplify, simplify, simplify! A hectic, complicated life leaves you no room to succeed in higher things.

Dedicate yourself to all the little creative acts of your day—therein lies your success.

Use the bricks people throw at you as the building blocks for your success.

We are what we repeatedly do. Excellence, therefore, is not an act but a habit.

Treasure your curiosity, for it is the mainspring of your creativity.

Stay curious. Even if you live to be a hundred, never lose that. It is the thing that will inspire you to get out of bed every morning.

May we be curious.

We owe the whole of modern science to our own insatiable curiosity. Science may not be much good at answering the question "Why?" but it produces endless amusing and useful answers to the question "How?"

Great things are not done by impulse, but by a series of small things brought together.

Vincent van Gogh

It is enormously stimulating to really listen, to really see.

When it comes to inspiration, there is no better source to turn to than nature.

The only drug we need is a sense of wonder at the artistry of this amazing universe.

With a mindful outlook your entire life can be filled with revelation.

Creativity may not be what you expected or even what you could have imagined; and that is what makes it so great.

Protect your creative time. Learn to say no to those things that steal your time away, and be brave. Give yourself time to create. That is all you need do.

A traveler without observation
is a bird without wings.

Saadi

Every work of art represents an
exploration of the mind.

You might work on several
projects at once. It is an amazing
quality of the mind that thinking
about one will inspire creative
thoughts about others.

Fine art is that in which the hand, the head, and the heart of man go together.

John Ruskin

Take any object. Touch it, feel its shape, really notice its colors, what it does—as if you have never before touched, felt, or observed it. With this awareness, creativity grows.

Have you every noticed how hard it is to express exactly what is on your mind? All art springs from this.

Let your body do the creating for you—your hands know what to do.

Creativity often arises from the part of the mind that is invisible. It may go against the grain to trust in what you can't see, but when you learn to do this, you can create anything.

The creation of something new is not accomplished by the intellect but by the play instinct acting from inner necessity. The creative mind plays with the objects it loves.

344

Let go of the known, the safe, the predictable. Open yourself to that which is most unexpected.

Creativity is expressing the connection between thoughts and experiences.

We are all creative— we just need to know this to be true.

Let this be your creativity mantra: Whatever I do is always good enough.

Let nature inspire you to create. Notice what nature makes.

No idea is
ever wasted.

When you're in the
creative flow, time has
no meaning; nothing
else exists.

Whatever you
love doing is your
creative work.

We are limited not by the place of our birth, nor the color of our skin, but by how much we allow ourselves to imagine and wonder.

Change your routines so every day brings a new experience that feeds your ideas. Walk or drive a new route, go to a different store, speak to someone you haven't spoken to before.

Where are you now? You are always in the perfect place to think creatively, because creativity is within you.

Laughter is a creative way to see another side of a situation.

Anything is possible. Your thinking makes it so.

Creativity is just connecting things. When you ask creative people how they did something, they feel a little guilty because they didn't really do it, they just saw something...

Steve Jobs

Everything is interesting.

By being mindful of every moment, we nurture our ability to create.

Decide what success means for you, not according to how anyone else defines it. If you don't define it, how will you know when it arrives?

7
The wisdom of patience

Restore your attention or bring it to a new level by dramatically slowing down whatever you're doing.

Sharon Salzberg

Relax and get to know yourself. Try to understand life and your part in it. But take it slowly.

Life is a gift—unwrap it carefully.

Patience comes into being when the brain discovers its fallibility and forgives itself.

It's not that I'm so smart, it's just that I stay with problems longer.

Albert Einstein

Don't mistake movement for achievement.

Attentive patience creates humility.

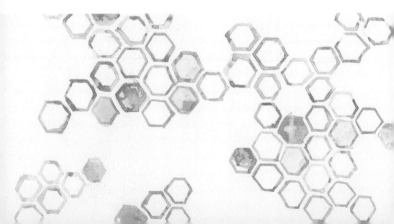

I long to accomplish great and noble tasks, but it is my chief duty to accomplish humble tasks as though they were great and noble. The world is moved along, not only by the mighty shoves of its heroes, but also by the aggregate of the tiny pushes of each honest worker.

Helen Keller

Patience is organic time.

Learning to remove all the haste in life allows you to find the essence of who you are.

On your way to wherever you are going, find beautiful things to notice.

It is a continual barrage of hurly-burly and urgency on which we all spend ourselves that keeps us from experiencing who we truly are.

Becoming who you are begins the process of finding your stillness among many.

Accept that there is no need
to rush yourself or others
in facing the challenges of
emotional growth.

You are surrounded by miracles, if
you take the time to look and feel
their presence.

Clear your mind of all the noise
and upheaval of the modern
world and make time stand still.

Slow down and pay attention to your thoughts.

Adopt the pace of nature: her secret is patience.

Ralph Waldo Emerson

Patience is an acceptance of how things are. Through acceptance, we begin to change our reality.

Slow down so that you may give and receive encouragement.

Haste often pursues those things that seem to be profitable for ourselves; pausing and saying "no" to this busyness helps us understand what is best for the general good.

Every aspect of the life of an individual and of the life of the world has its own pace.

There's nothing wrong with standing still; a rock that stands unmoved amid the constantly moving waves of the sea of life becomes a rock for others to lean on, to depend upon.

Slow down and allow yourself to see the best in others.

Nature speaks to us through its rhythms, its seasons. The leaves fall when they will. Shoots emerge when they will.

When in doubt, slow down.

Persistence is active patience.

If we were to live patiently, our lives may heal themselves.

A person can succeed at almost anything with which he has unlimited patience.

Patience affords you the space to generate your own circumstances.

The storm is only temporary.
What creates a lasting
impression is the marvel you
experience when the sun bursts
through the clouds and begins
to shine once more.

Great patience takes
great courage.

Patience cannot heal
sorrows, but it makes
them lighter to bear.

Time is a created thing. To say,
"I don't have time," is like saying,
"I don't want to."

Lao Tzu

You have time
to be patient.

Infinite patience
brings immediate
results.

Wayne Dyer

The most beautiful
things in the world reveal
themselves slowly.

Treasure every
moment; it won't
come again.

Don't just do something;
sit there.

Kiva Bottero

The next time you
want something to
fall into your lap, try
sitting down.

No mountain is too big for you to move. Just pick up one stone at a time.

I'm a slow walker, but I never walk back.

Abraham Lincoln

Impatience is concerned with how quickly we move toward our goal. Patience is concerned with how we move toward our goal.

Do not worry; eat three square meals a day; say your prayers; be courteous to your creditors; keep your digestion good; exercise; go slow and easy.

I used to work in publishing. Authors would pester the Managing Director for a decision on their books. Little did they know that his Number 1 rule was: "The quick answer is always 'No.'"

In your haste you walk far too fast. And in doing so you often leave your soul behind.

To be patient with another is to show simple human courtesy.

Patience is a form of wisdom. It demonstrates that we understand and accept the fact that sometimes things must unfold in their own time.

Jon Kabat-Zinn

Compassion is the basis of patience.

Take your time. To be in a hurry is to kill your talent. If you wish to reach the sun it isn't enough to jump impulsively into the air.

Peter Ustinov

Be patient with the present.

Like visitors, be patient with your thoughts; welcome then in, invite them to tea, but tell them when it's time to go.

The sea does not reward those who are too anxious, too greedy, or too impatient. To dig for treasures shows not only impatience and greed, but also lack of faith. Patience, patience, patience, is what the sea teaches. Patience and faith. One should lie empty, open, choiceness as a beach—waiting for a gift from the sea.

Anne Morrow Lindbergh

Patience frees us to act according to the circumstances, rather than our expectations.

Calmness is ours if we choose to adopt the pace of nature, for nature's secret is her patience.

Is it harder to wait than to work?

Patience allows you to find some peace despite the difficulties of life, rather than to postpone well-being until after you have conquered all your troubles.

Patience is the understanding of and participation in diversity.

Replace all your worry with patience, because although your patience may not solve all your problems, worry won't solve any of them.

Patience serves as a protection against wrongs as clothes do against cold. For if you put on more clothes as the cold increases, it will have no power to hurt you. So in like manner you must grow in patience when you meet with great wrongs, and they will then be powerless to vex your mind.

Leonardo da Vinci

Patience is the best remedy for every trouble.

Tackle a job
with impatience
and it will take
twice as long.

The mind may march forward slowly, but it never stops.

The tortoise beat the hare through his persistence. It's a cliché, but clichés have truth. Patience can win.

An ounce of patience is worth a pound of brains.

Dutch proverb

When you slow down, you notice what's catching you up.

Our friends are the garden in which we plant our trust, our hope, our love, and our faith and in which we give thanks for each blossom, however much time it may take to bloom.

Slow down and you'll see the things that matter the most.

Sometimes in life we feel anxious—one becomes fearful of looking forward or backward. That is when we realize that if we look beside us there is just the present, patiently waiting for us to say hello.

Busy does not mean important. It just means you don't have time to laugh.

Have a day of slow-tech. Write letters. Wash by hand. Walk. Sweep the floor. Read a little.

Go at your pace and be patient with yourself, and you allow everyone else to be comfortable too.

Just breathe.

You don't need an immediate answer for anything.

Why is patience so important? Because it makes us pay attention.

Paulo Coelho

Being patient can feel
uncomfortable. Allow the
discomfort. Then ask it
what you need to do.

When you are patient with yourself,
you give yourself time to consider,
time to be aware, time to make the
most of every opportunity.

When you show patience to
others, you show them respect.

When you're next waiting in a queue, don't click onto the track labeled "irritation." When else would you have an opportunity to stop what you're doing and look around you?

Cultivating patience is like growing an extra heart.

Our patience will achieve more than our force.

Edmund Burke

With patience a ruler may be persuaded, and a soft tongue will break a bone.

Proverbs 25:15

Patience is mindful waiting.

Patience is not inaction;
it is taking time to
quietly consider all
aspects of a thing.

Impatience is one way to
stop a thing happening.

If you are waiting
impatiently, it's not
patience, but tolerance.

When we are patient, we show our trust in the outcome.

When we are patient, we surrender to life, believing that it knows best.

When we are patient, we are kind.

When we hurtle from one thing to the next, we miss out on the beauty that is right in front of us.

Patience requires self-control. With self-control comes the wisdom that experience brings.

Whoever restrains his words has knowledge, and he who has a cool spirit is a man of understanding.

Proverbs 17:27

Slow time feeds the creative self.

When you can avoid finishing other people's sentences, you really begin to hear what they have to say.

When you don't rehearse your next sentence, you're really taking the time to listen.

Patience is listening to someone talk about himself or herself when you want to talk about yourself.

For one day, vow not to interrupt anyone's conversation. Can you do this?

For one day, vow to listen more than you talk. Can you do this?

For one day, vow to consider problems rather than fix them. Can you do this?

Don't rush to judge. Rash judgment is a lack of attention.

A fool gives full vent to his spirit, but a wise man quietly holds it back.

Proverbs 29:11

If we spent half an hour every day in silent immobility, I am convinced that we should conduct all our affairs, personal, national, and international, far more sanely than we do at present.

Bertrand Russell

Take your time. What's the hurry?

God grant me
patience... now!

**Enjoy the process,
not the goal.**

Slow down and smell
the coffee.

Can you stop—now?

Every seed
knows its time—
all in good time.
Russian proverb

Patience expands
time so we have
more of it.

Computers are incredibly fast,
accurate, and stupid; humans
are incredibly slow, inaccurate,
and brilliant; together they are
powerful beyond imagination.

Albert Einstein

My brother is really, really slow.

Usain Bolt

8
Living with awareness

Mindfulness and awareness is
the bridge between reaction and
conscious choice.

Hal Tipper

Like a child standing in a beautiful
park with his eyes shut tight, there's
no need to imagine trees, flowers,
deer, birds, and sky; we merely need
to open our eyes and realize what is
already here, who we already are—as
soon as we stop pretending we're
small or unholy.

Bo Lozoff

To be more mindful, one should simply choose to be. Then be. Then support everyone else in being.

A Native American grandfather was talking to his grandson about how he felt. He said, "I feel as if I have two wolves fighting in my heart. One wolf is the vengeful, angry one. The other wolf is the loving, compassionate one." The grandson asked him, "Which wolf will win the fight in your heart?" The grandfather answered, "The one I feed."

Awareness is joyful.

Awareness is acceptance.

Awareness is love.

The senses are the
foundation for a life of
awareness.

While some think that holding on makes us strong, sometimes it all comes down to letting go.

There is comfort to be gained from being able to accept that there are some things that cannot be changed.

Imagine the happiness of knowing that you do not necessarily require happiness.

Mindfulness is that space where you are in touch with life-experience and you are brightly aware.

Bryant H McGill

Pleasure denied remains pleasure sought. Take care of your needs now.

Our responsibility to ourselves is to awaken, to become acutely aware of everything around us, in each moment as it arises.

"There's a light at the end of the tunnel," says the optimist.
"It's probably a train coming straight at us," says the pessimist.
But there is only a light, a train, and a tunnel.

Paradise is where
you are; paradise lost
is where you are not.

A hopeful heart
and an open
mind are the
best traveling
companions.

Don't always be running to something, or from something. Sometimes just run.

Allow your mind to settle—like the muddy water churned up by a boat, it will soon become clear when undisturbed.

Accept people just how they are, rather than expect people to be the way we want them to be.

Use the gift of sight—
don't miss a thing
and share the joys
with others.

The best journeys
are not always in
straight lines.

A world full of suffering is also a world full of people overcoming their suffering.

Where you are, with what you have, do what you can.

Let us dare to live our life as we understand it.

There's absolutely nothing we can do when our car is stuck in traffic or our flight is overdue. Take the opportunity to relax and take a look at life around you.

Are you comfortable with who you are?

I'll be old when I feel like it.

When we are true
to nature, we can be
comfortable with our age.

Age is not half as
important as attitude.

I intend never to feel as old as I am.

To someone celebrating their 100th birthday, anyone under the age of 90 is young.

Whatever your reflection tells you, the spirit does not grow old.

Learning to love your enemies always sounds hopelessly idealistic, but it isn't really. One thing your enemies do is to show you yourself through a distorting glass. It can be an informative experience.

If we were all comfortable with who we are, we'd only ever have to buy the things we really need and like.

Do everything with intent, and know that every little thing you do is important.

Live your life on all its levels:
Your physical life,
Your mental life,
Your emotional life,
And your spiritual life.

The right to mismanage your affairs is a freedom in itself.

You can do small things in a great way.

Begin each day with a sense of wonder.

Begin each day with an openness to love.

Begin each day with an openness to learn.

Begin each day mindful of every moment.

Despite everything, mountains are mountains, waters are waters.

Even if we do nothing at all, the spring arrives and the grass grows.

Everything is just as it is.

Rain will fall; we cannot make it so.

Every day there is the chance to learn something new.

For your own sake, learn to forgive those who have offended you.

A wise man will make haste to forgive, because he knows the true value of time, and will not suffer it to pass away in unnecessary pain.

Samuel Johnson

To be wronged is nothing unless you choose to remember it.

Forgive yourself for your imperfections. It's perfectly fine to be imperfect.

Make forgiveness your constant, unswerving companion.

Instead of pointing a finger, may you hold out your hands.

If you have been wronged, let it go. Forgive for your sake as well as theirs.
He who is devoid of the power to forgive is devoid of the power to love.

Martin Luther King Jr

We can only forgive to the extent to which we love.

As I walked out the door toward the gate that would lead to my freedom, I knew if I didn't leave my bitterness and hatred behind, I'd still be in prison.

Nelson Mandela

There are five steps in learning:
Silence
Listening
Accepting
Practicing
Teaching others.

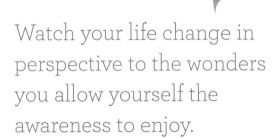

Watch your life change in
perspective to the wonders
you allow yourself the
awareness to enjoy.

How many
possibilities do you
see when you look
around your world?

It is good to ask "Why?",
but it is even better to ask
"Why not?" because that is
when we allow the magic
to happen.

Whatever life hands you, good or bad, is still a gift.

Seeking the source of the river leads you away from the sea. Stay where you are and enjoy the water.

A willingness to accept can often be the first step to effecting change.

When you judge others, you don't define them; you define yourself.

We are disturbed not by things, but by the attitude we take towards them.

Those who annoy us most are often our greatest teachers.

Awareness of our talents gives us the ability to transform problems into opportunities.

When you set out on a journey and fog covers the road, you don't decide that the road has vanished forever. The road exists still; be patient and the fog will disperse.

Self-awareness is both a sign and a generator of positive self-esteem.

Everything is not always about you.

Rather than ask, "Why did this happen to me?" you might inquire, "Why was I selected for this opportunity?"

You don't need to make promises to your future self. The pleasure in life is now; you are worthy of joy just as you are.

When you are truly ready for an experience, it comes to you. All you need do is notice its arrival.

Do not place all that you want in the future—time, money, or other improved circumstances; there is much to gain from seeing what you have now, this moment.

As far as possible, be mindful of the long-term consequences of your actions by doing what feels right, right now.

Remove the expectation from what you give and share.

Self-awareness enables us to act spontaneously rather than on our fears.

Mindfulness is an attitude we can cultivate. We become mindful by being present in our lives moment by moment; the way we experience our moments is the way we spend our lives.

Take your troubles, and let them teach you.

Be open, and you will learn new things at any time in your life.

Patience enables us, in every situation, to answer the demands of the moment.

The eye sees only what the mind is patient enough to comprehend.

People are always more than they seem.

We find what we look for. Look for the best in others and yourself.

When you become aware of inauthenticity in others, do not draw attention to it; observe with passive detachment and prefer forgiveness to judgment.

Nature gave us one tongue and two ears so we could hear twice as much as we speak.

Epictetus

Change is unavoidable and inevitable. Patience helps us to accept the truth of transience.

Impatience criticizes the growing conditions; patience sows the seeds of change.

Pay more
attention
to the good
stuff.

441

The mind is like water. Thrash around in it and you will only stir up the mud. Just let it settle of its own accord.

Your own nature is fundamentally clean and pure.

A pot is empty, yet that emptiness is the whole point of the pot.

Zen monks meditate with their eyes slightly open because what they are concerned with is right in front of them.

The world is like a mirror.
See? Smile, and your friends smile back.

Zen saying

When you meditate do not expect miracles or magic, but expect (slowly, slowly) to see everyday life as it really is.

It is said that when the pupil is ready the teacher appears. Of course, you have to recognize the teacher.

Normal life carries on without people noticing just how extraordinary it is.

Sit quietly and wait. Let things happen, and you will know when to act and when to leave well alone.

The wild geese do not mean to cast a reflection,
The water has no intention of receiving their image.

Zenrin Kushu

You do not need improving. When you understand that, you will be much improved.

Sell your cleverness and buy bewilderment. Cleverness is mere opinion; bewilderment is intuition.

Rumi

If you don't meditate, learn. It's easy. It won't interfere with whatever beliefs you hold and it can improve your life by several hundred percent.

Being busy isn't always the best use of your energy. Contemplate, then act.

It's remarkable how much effort people will expend to get things they don't need.

You don't need to think of yourself as fully finished. Like a snake, you can always split your skin and grow a bit more.

When you run out of known paths, the wild country is revealed in its splendor.

All that is not eternal is eternally out of date.

C S Lewis

I was once introduced to Geraldine as a psychologist. During the whole meeting, although I said little, she was clearly nervous. Later, when we knew each other better she confided that throughout the meeting she'd been unable to see any further than that one word.

When we truly know and love ourselves we step into our power.

You don't need to seek paths. Paths are made by walking.

If you can be happy
while you wait
for a late bus on a
rainy morning, then
you've figured it
out.

Perfect happiness is the absence
of striving for happiness.

Chuang-Tzu

Laugh now, even before you are happy, and perhaps happiness will follow.

Happiness is not at the destination but in the flowers that you smell along the way.

Happiness can be found in what seems trivial, the everyday stuff of life— a falling leaf, snow, a fly.

Now is the time to be content. This is the place to be aware of your contentment.

If only we'd stop striving to be happy we'd have a pretty good time.

Edith Wharton

Happy is he who has curiosity.

Die when I may, I want it said by those who knew me best that I always plucked a thistle and planted a flower where I thought a flower would grow.

Abraham Lincoln

When any glassy-eyed zealot promises to make you happy, chase him out of town. Happiness is gentle and eschews fanatics.

Always have an open mind—you need plenty of places for happiness to get in.

Sometimes happiness is just like a cat. Go and offer to be friends and it will run away, but sit down and feign disinterest and nothing will stop it from rubbing up against your legs.

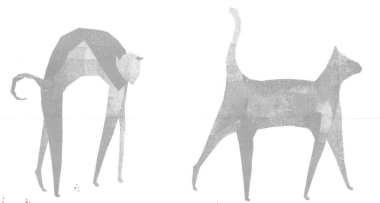

Happiness is not a goal in itself—it is a side effect of living your life with true awareness.

The mere sense of living is joy enough.

Emily Dickinson

Life delights in life.

William Blake

Happiness is like listening to music. The object is to enjoy it from minute to minute, not to race through it to get to the end as soon as possible.

Plenty of people are happy without having the least idea that they are.

Mindfulness meditation doesn't change life. Life remains as fragile and unpredictable as ever. Meditation changes the heart's capacity to accept life as it is. It teaches the heart to be more accommodating, not by beating it into submission, but by making it clear that accommodation is a gratifying choice.

Sylvia Boorstein

There are two ways to wash dishes:
One is to wash them in order to
make them clean; the other is to
wash them in order to wash them.

Anthony de Mello

**The miracle is not to walk on
water. The miracle is to walk
on earth.**

Take pleasure in the art of living
daily: really dine—prepare, cook,
and savor.

Each day is full
of opportunities;
it is your job to
recognize them.

Mindfulness is
a presence, an
awareness that
we all can share.

A little change in daily routine can help us appreciate our lives more—anything from changing the color of your bath towel to taking a different route to work.

Observe the world with care, and accept what you see as a gift, without judgment.

Occasionally you might have to tell white lies to others if only to spare their feelings, but always be honest with yourself.

You need only the approval of your self.

What happens to you in life is not that important. What you do with what happens is the important part.